The Cheerios Counting Book

by Barbara Barbieri McGrath
Illustrated by Rob Bolster and Frank Mazzola, Jr.

Cartwheel
·B·O·O·K·S·®
SCHOLASTIC INC.

New York   Toronto   London   Auckland   Sydney

Text copyright © 1998 by Barbara Barbieri McGrath.
Illustrations copyright © 1998 by Rob Bolster and Frank Mazzola, Jr.

Cheerios is a registered trademark of General Mills, Inc. used under license
by Corporate Board Books, Natick, Massachusetts, 01760.

Library of Congress Cataloging-in-Publication Data

McGrath, Barbara Barbieri
      The Cheerios counting book/ by Barbara Barbieri McGrath;
   illustrated by Rob Bolster and Frank Mazzola, Jr.
         p.   cm.
      Summary: Text and illustrations of the familiar O-shaped cereal help
   the reader count to ten and add groups of ten.
      ISBN 0-590-00321-6
      1. Counting — Juvenile literature. [1. Counting.   2. Arithmetic.]
   1. Bolster, Rob, ill. ll. Mazzola, Frank, ill. lll. Title.
   QA113.M393684   1998
   513.2'11— dc21
   [E]   97-52819
                                                                     CIP
                                                                      AC

10 9 8 7 6 5 4 3 2   8 9/9 0/0 01 02 03

Printed in Mexico   49
First printing, September 1998

The author and illustrators would like to **dedicate** this book with gratitude to —
Jerry Pallotta

Special thanks *to Will McGrath, Corporate Board Books; Deb Thorpe and Kim Walter, General Mills; and Gina Shaw and Edith Weinberg, Cartwheel Books, for their ideas, support, and efforts.*

– B. M.
– R. B.
– F. M.

1one

You can count cereal.
What fun it will be!
See **one**.

two

Here are **two**.

3 three

Now there are **three**.

four

Take another **O** from your mix.

See **four**.

 **five**

Here are **five**.

six **6**

Now there are **six**.

7
seven

You can count cereal.
You're counting just fine.
See seven.

eight

Here are **eight**.

9
nine

Now there are nine.

ten **10**

To reach the next number, take an **O** again.
Count one, two, three, four, five,
six, seven, eight, nine, **ten**.

 **11** eleven

 **12** twelve

 **13** thirteen

 **14** fourteen

 **15** fifteen

 **16** sixteen

 **17** seventeen

 **18** eighteen

 **19** nineteen

20
twenty

Let's keep counting **O**'s. There sure are plenty.
Eleven, twelve, thirteen, fourteen, fifteen,
sixteen, seventeen, eighteen, nineteen,
twenty!

10

ten

Now, with groups of **ten**,
to one hundred you'll count.
One hundred is a large amount!

20

twenty

Here are two groups of ten.

That makes **twenty** for you.

30

thirty

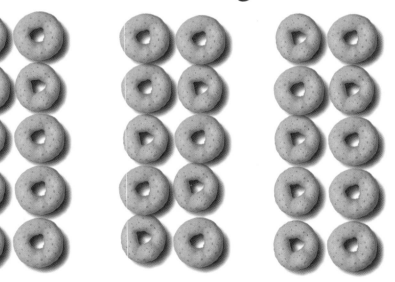

Three groups make **thirty**.

That's easy to do.

40

forty

Now there are forty. Count each group.
There are four.

50
fifty

Five groups are fifty.
You just added ten more.

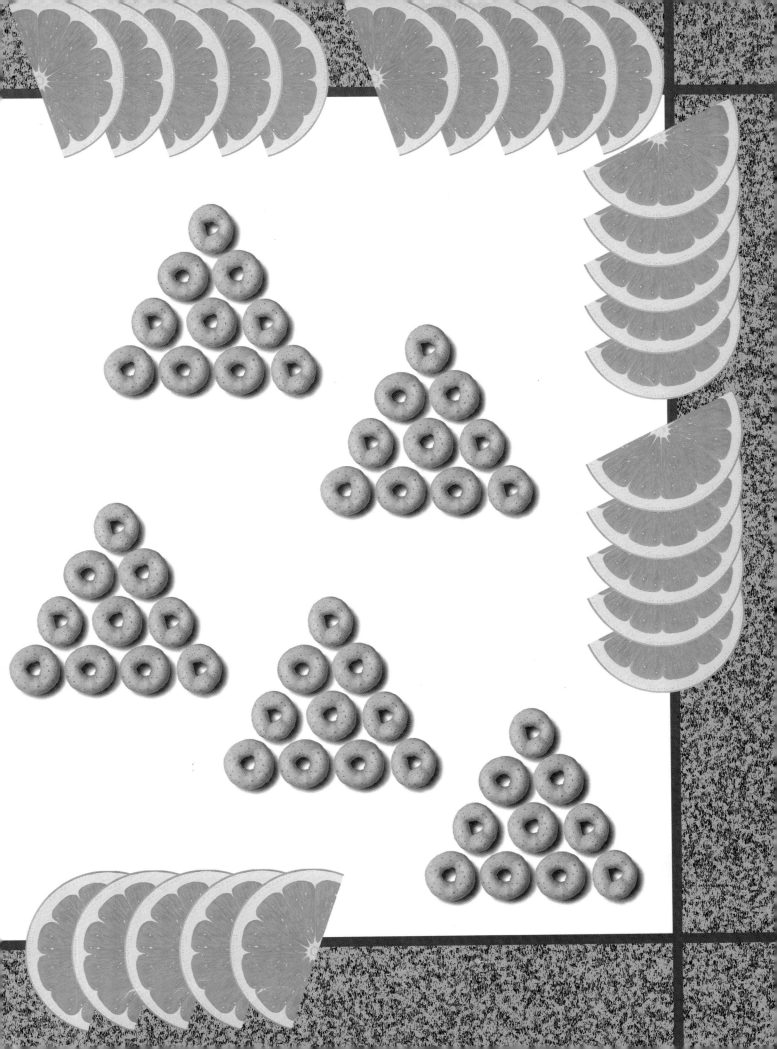

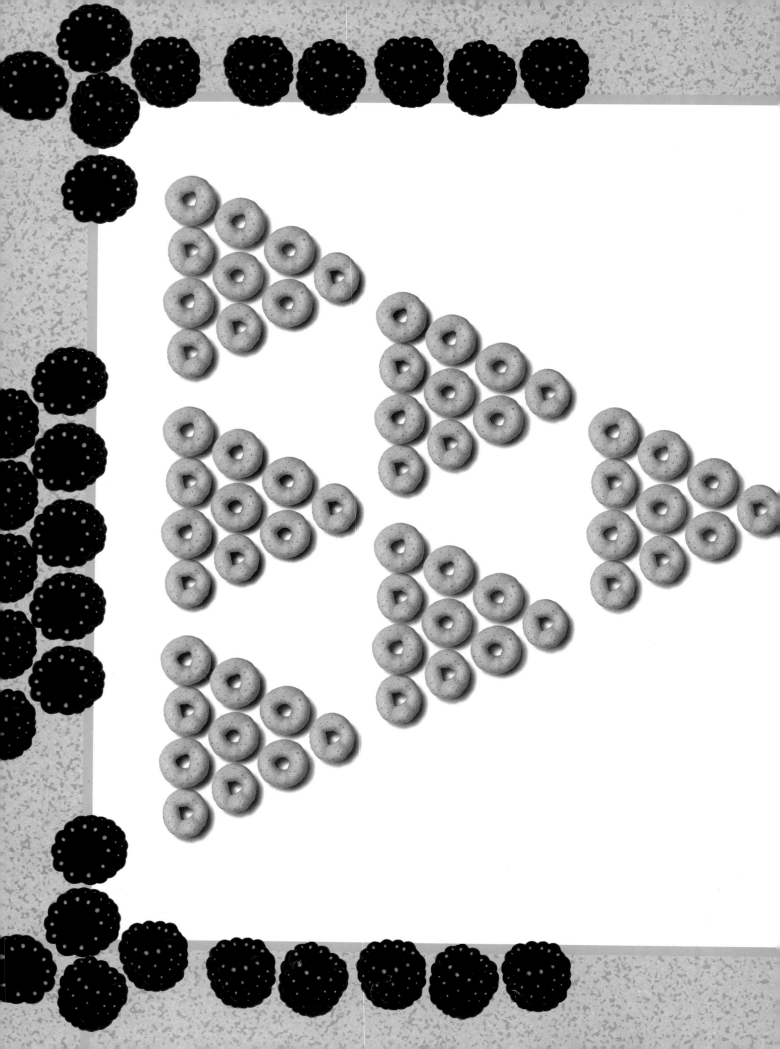

60

sixty

Sixty is six groups with ten in each bunch.

70
seventy

See seventy.
Seven groups that you could munch!

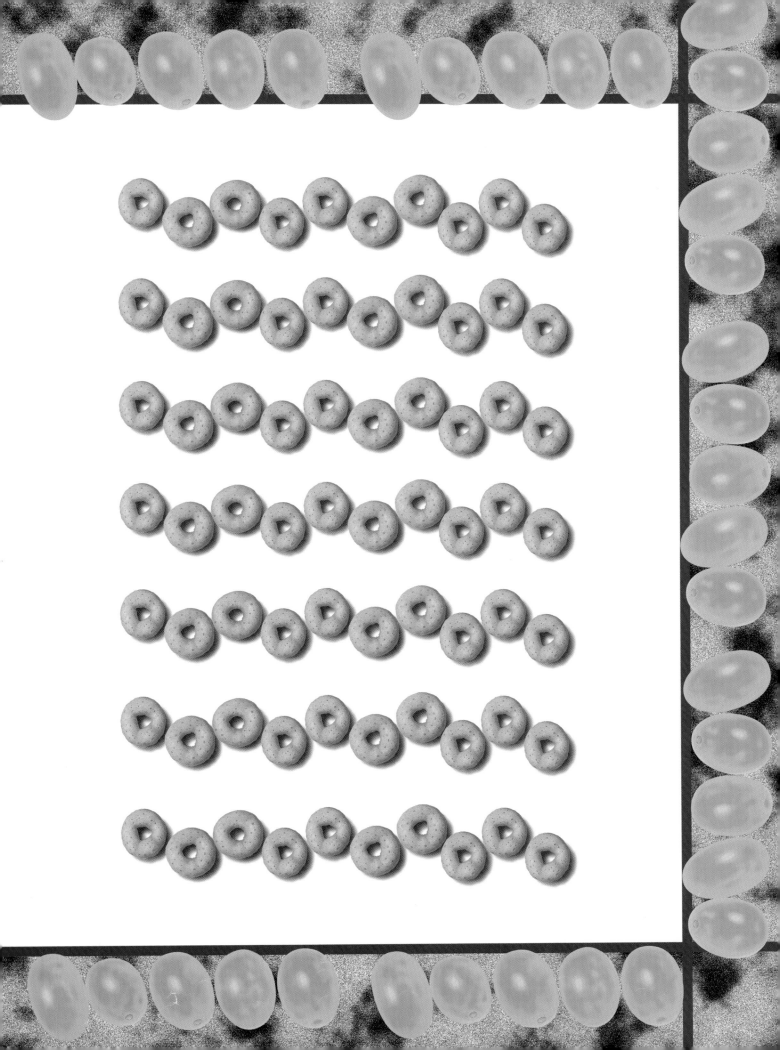

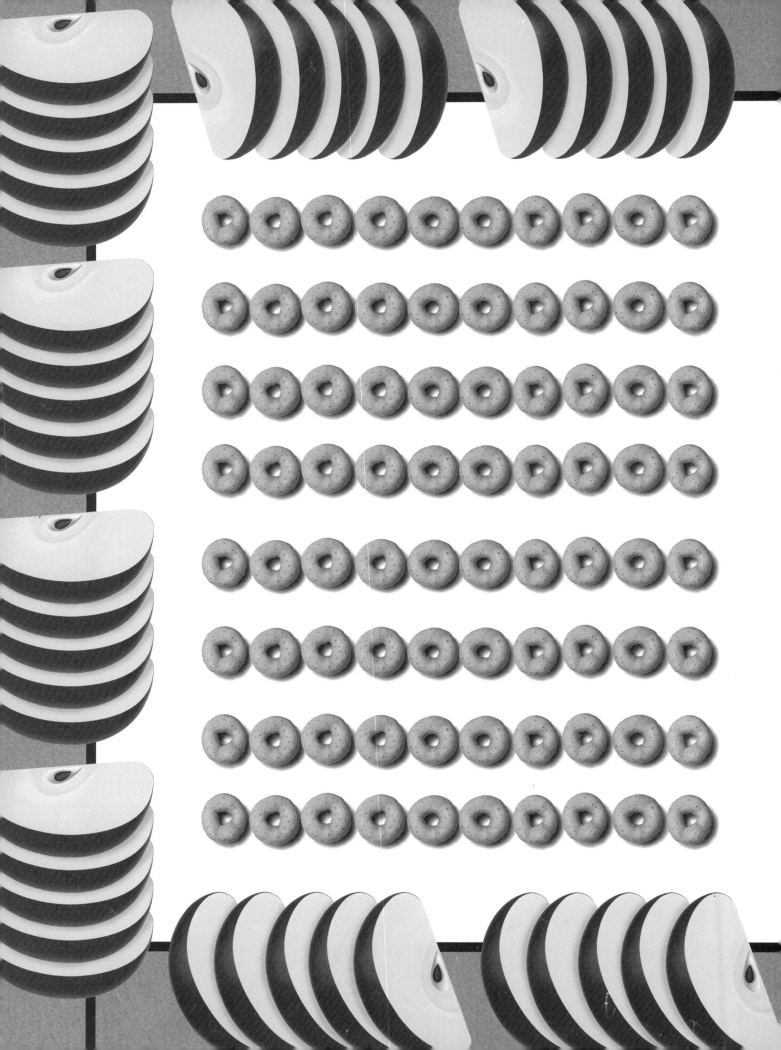

80

eighty

To count to **eighty**,
eight tens there will be.

90
ninety

Here's **ninety**.
That's nine tens. They're easy to see!

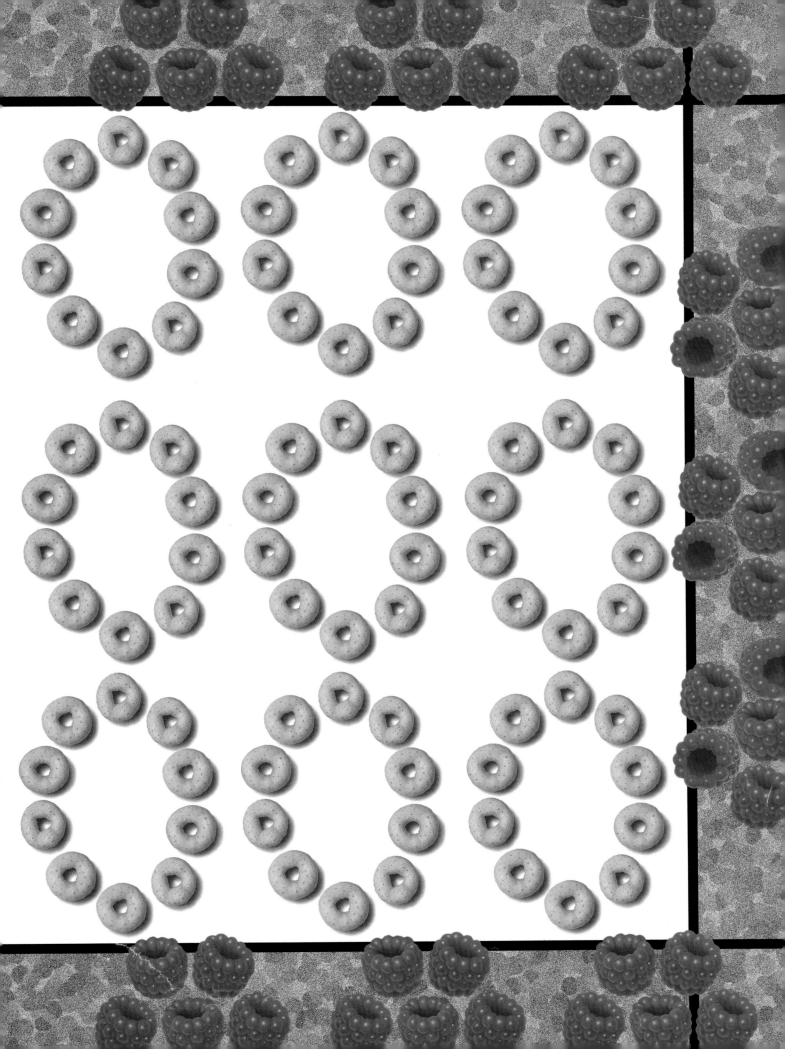

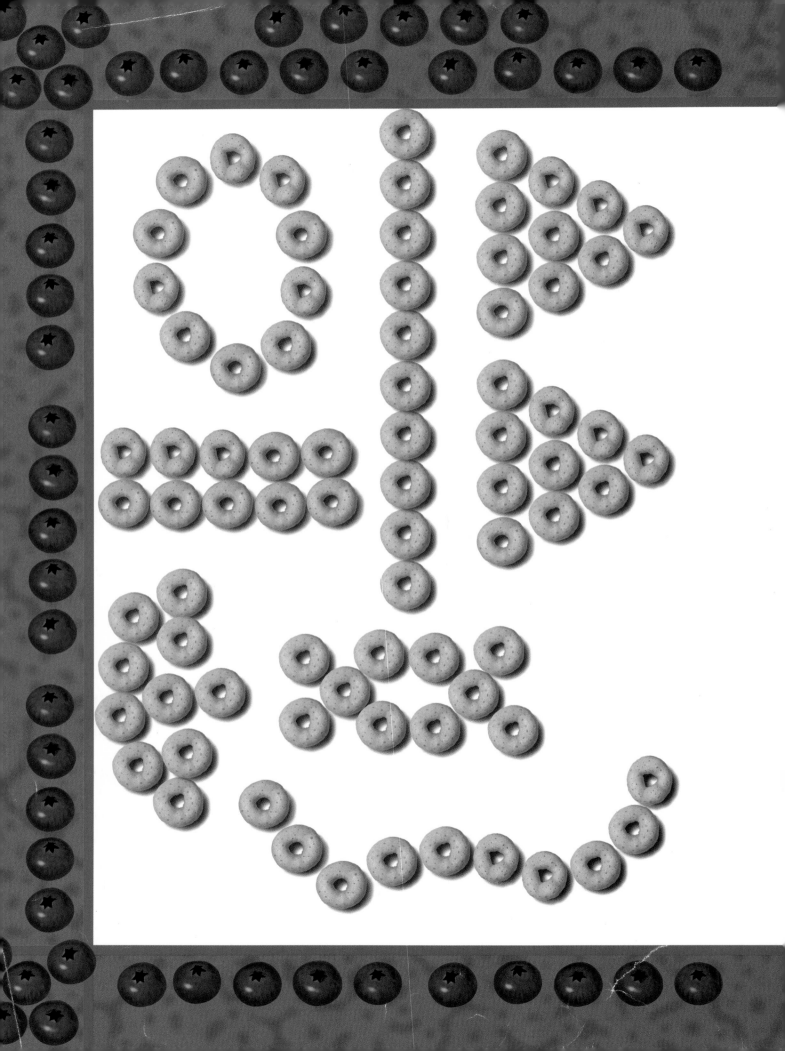

100
one hundred

Ten groups of ten make a special treat.
Now you have **one hundred O**'s to eat!

zero

Counting with cereal has really been fun.
Zero is the number you get
when you're done!